ACTION SPORTS

SNOWBOARDING

Joe Herran and Ron Thomas

This edition first published in 2003 in the United States of America by Chelsea House Publishers, a subsidiary of Haights Cross Communications.

Reprinted 2003

Chelsea House Publishers
1974 Sproul Road, Suite 400
Broomall, PA 19008-0914

The Chelsea House world wide web address is www.chelseahouse.com

Library of Congress Cataloging-in-Publication Data

Herran, Joe.
Snowboarding / by Joe Herran and Ron Thomas.
v. cm. — (Action sports)

Includes index.
Contents: What is snowboarding? — Snowboarding gear — Snowboarding safely — Maintaining the snowboard — Skills, tricks and techniques — A snowboarding interview — In competition — Snowboarding champions —Then and now — Related action sports.

ISBN 0-7910-7003-4
1. Snowboarding—Juvenile literature. [1. Snowboarding.] I. Thomas, Ron, 1947- II. Title. III. Action sports (Chelsea House Publishers)
GV857.S57 H47 2003
796.9—dc21

2002002296

First published in 2002 by
MACMILLAN EDUCATION AUSTRALIA PTY LTD
627 Chapel Street, South Yarra, Australia, 3141

Edited by Miriana Dasovic
Text design by Karen Young
Cover design by Karen Young
Illustrations by Nives Porcellato and Andy Craig
Page layout by Raul Diche
Photo research by Legend Images

Printed in China

Acknowledgements
The authors wish to acknowledge and thank Marcus Zeuschner for his assistance and advice in the writing of this text.

Cover photo: Snowboarder, courtesy of Sport the library.

Australian Picture Library/Corbis, pp. 5 (top), 12, 13 (bottom), 30; Australian Picture Library/Empics, p. 24 (top); Australian Picture Library/Picture Book, p. 18 (top); Burton, pp. 7, 8, 9 (bottom), 11 (bottom), 13 (top), 15 (right), 19 (bottom), 28, 29 (left); Getty Images/Allsport, pp. 26, 27 (left), 29 (right); Getty Images/ Photodisc, pp. 11 (top), 21 (right); photolibrary.com, p. 20 (bottom); Dale Mann/Retrospect, pp. 6, 14–15; Reuters, p. 25 (right); Sport the library, pp. 4, 5 (center and bottom), 16, 17, 19 (top), 21 (left), 24 (bottom), 25 (left), 27 (right); Ron Thomas, pp. 9 (top), 10, 22 (left); Marcus Zeuschner, pp. 22–23.

While every care has been taken to trace and acknowledge copyright the publisher tenders their apologies for any accidental infringement where copyright has proved untraceable.

CONTENTS

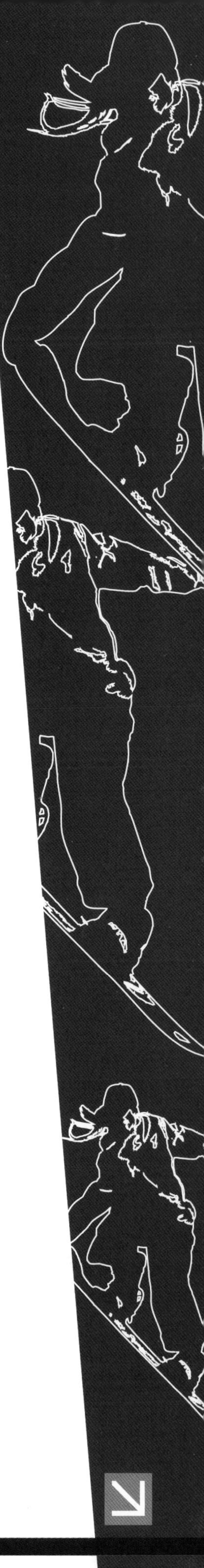

INTRODUCTION

In this book you will read about:

- snowboards and how they are made
- the gear used by snowboarders
- the safety measures used to keep snowboarders safe
- the basic skills, tricks and stunts of snowboarding
- some of the top snowboarders in competition today
- the history of the sport from its beginnings in the 1960s.

In the beginning

Snowboarding began in the 1960s when Sherman Poppen built the first snowboard for his daughter and called it the Snurfer. It looked like a cross between a plywood sled and a skateboard deck. A handheld rope was attached to the **nose** of the board to give the snowboarder something to hold on to. There were also steel tacks that poked through the board to hold the snowboarder's feet in place.

Snowboarding today

Snowboarding is now a popular sport. Spectators thrill to the **slalom** races and the twists and spins of the competitors in the halfpipes made of snow. Street-style sliding and leaping over obstacles is also great fun.

Competitions attracting hundreds of professional and **amateur** competitors, male and female, are held in countries around the world. Snowboard design is constantly improving. Special shoes and clothing have been designed and made for snowboarders. Extreme or X Games featuring snowboarding have become popular events on television. In 1998, snowboarding was one of the new sports added to the Winter Olympic Games at Nagano, Japan.

This is not a how-to book for aspiring snowboarders. It is intended as an introduction to the exciting world of snowboarding and a look at where the sport has come from and where it is heading.

WHAT IS SNOWBOARDING?

Snowboarding is gliding over the snow with feet strapped to a board. There are three main styles of snowboarding: alpine racing or slalom, freestyle and freeriding.

Alpine racing or slalom

Alpine racing or slalom has the snowboarders racing down a hill or mountain, zigzagging and changing direction quickly to pass in and out of posts, called gates.

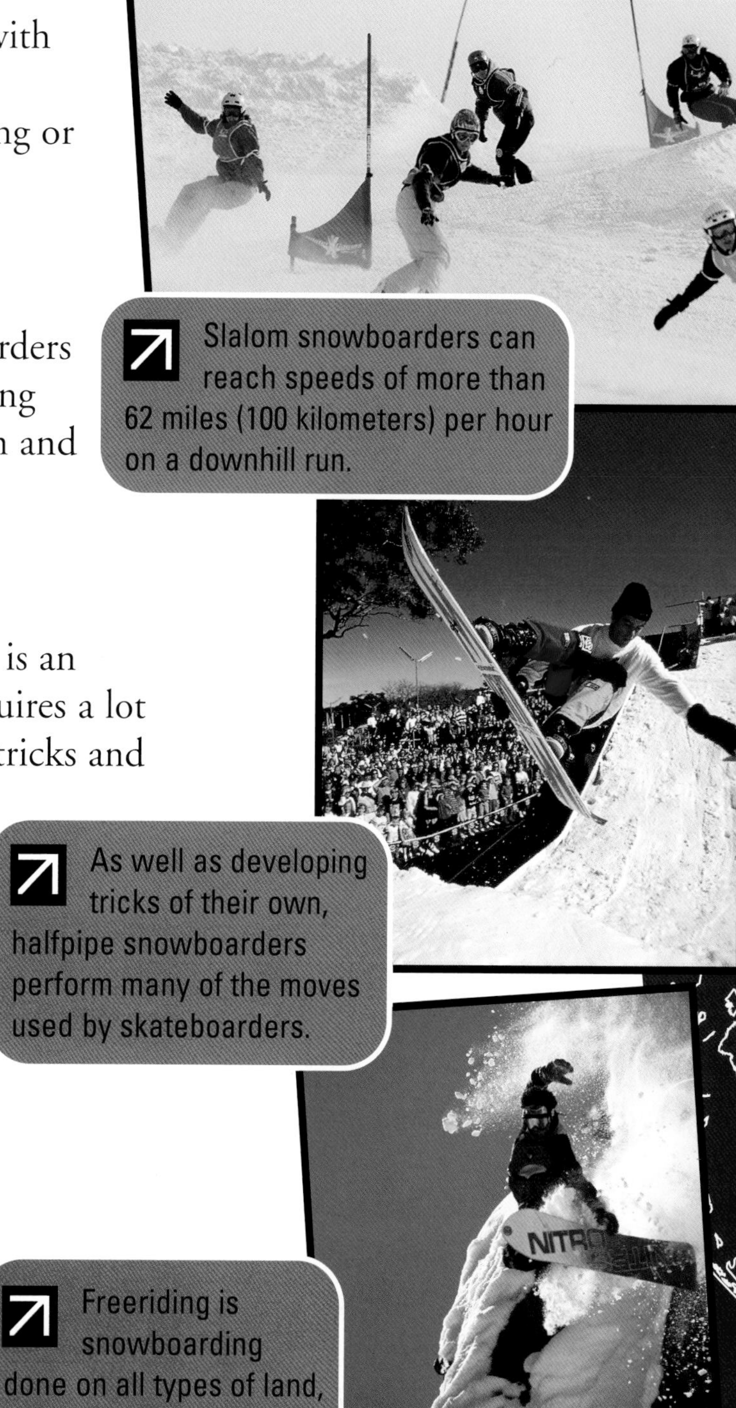

Slalom snowboarders can reach speeds of more than 62 miles (100 kilometers) per hour on a downhill run.

Freestyle

Freestyle racing includes the **halfpipe**. It is an acrobatic form of snowboarding that requires a lot of skill. Freestyle snowboarders perform tricks and jumps on flat ground or on and over rails, benches and boxes.

Halfpipe snowboarders perform tricks in a halfpipe cut into the snow. The snowboarder drops-in to the halfpipe, then rides to the top of the wall to perform tricks in the air above the halfpipe.

As well as developing tricks of their own, halfpipe snowboarders perform many of the moves used by skateboarders.

Freeriding

Freeriding snowboarders are not confined to resorts. They may use different styles of snowboarding as they explore the countryside.

Freeriding is snowboarding done on all types of land, not just halfpipes and groomed slopes.

SNOWBOARDING GEAR

The snowboard

All snowboards taper, or get narrower, toward the middle of the board. This taper is called the sidecut. The width of the board at its narrowest point is called waist width. The edges are made of sharp stainless steel to give the board strength and to cut into the snow. All boards have stainless steel inserts to hold the bindings in place.

The design of snowboards is constantly changing to meet the needs of snowboarders, who keep trying new tricks and experimenting with riding techniques.

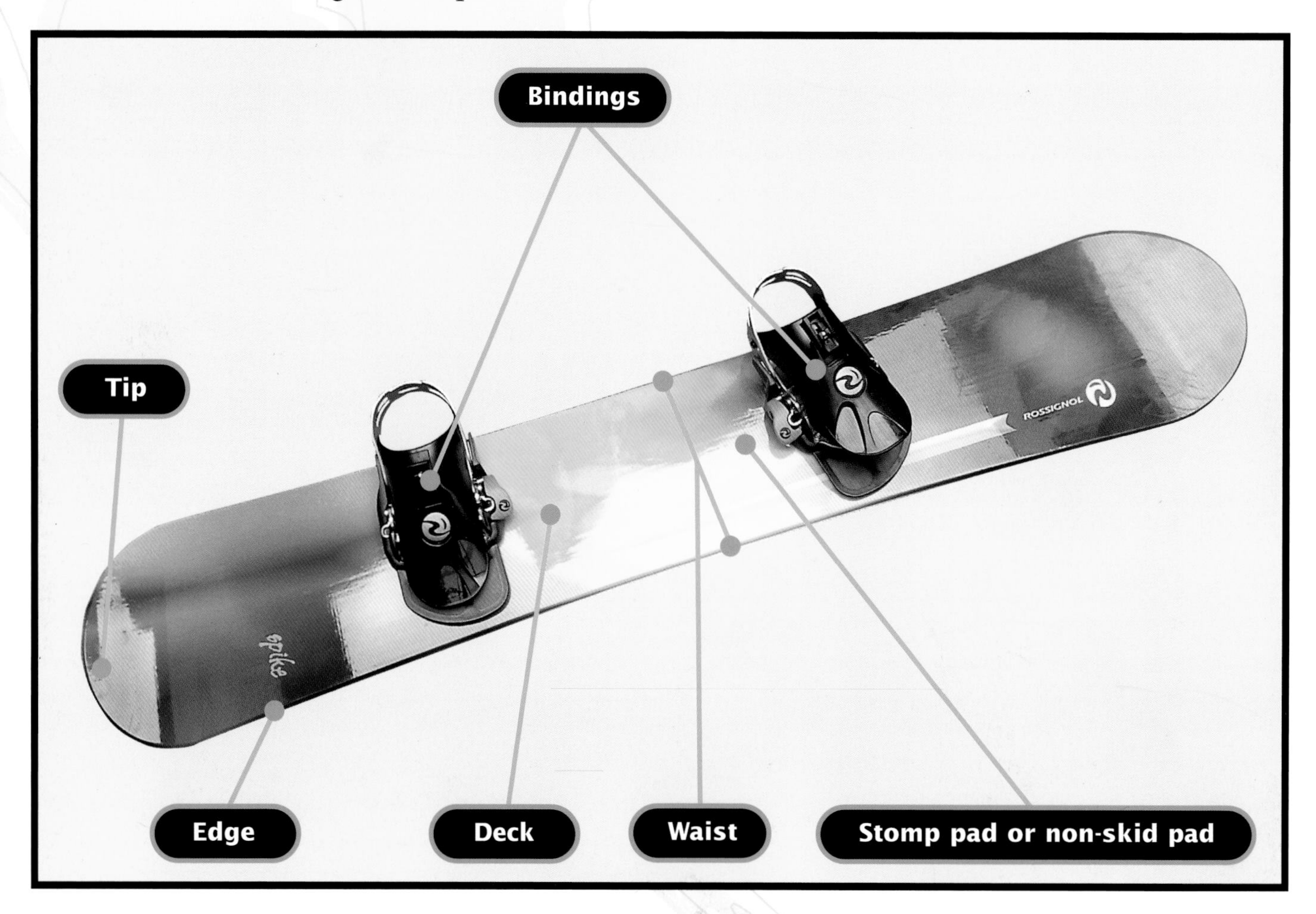

Alpine racing boards

Alpine racing boards are about 180 centimeters (71 inches) long. They have narrow waists, less than 25 centimeters (10 inches) wide. This makes them fast. The sidecut allows the racing snowboarder to make sharp turns at high speeds on tightly packed snow.

Freestyle or halfpipe boards

Freestyle boards are 130 to 150 centimeters (about 51 to 59 inches) long. They have less taper or sidecut than racing boards, with waists 26.5 to 28 centimeters (about $10\frac{1}{2}$ to 11 inches) wide. The boards are flexible and designed for performing jumps, spins and slides in the halfpipe. They have an upturned nose, and a tail called a kick at each end. The kick allows the rider to easily travel forwards or backwards.

Freeriding boards

Freeriding boards are built to allow snowboarders to move around in deep or compacted snow as they explore different parts of a mountain.

↗ Alpine racing boards are longer, flatter, stiffer and stronger than freestyle boards.

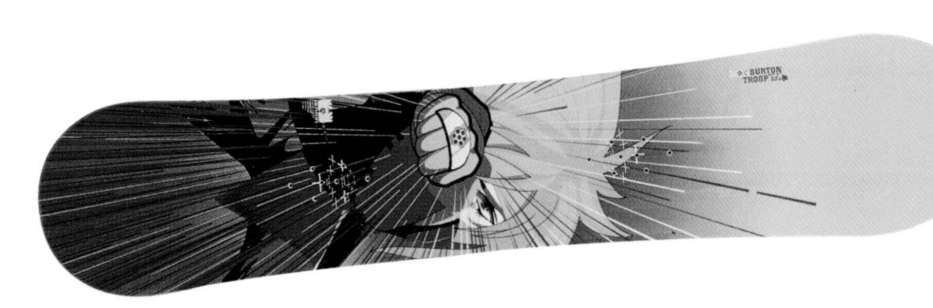

↙ Freestyle or halfpipe boards are shorter, fatter and lighter than racing boards.

↗ Freeriding boards are longer and narrower than freestyle boards.

Making a snowboard

Making the core

The core is the central part of a snowboard around which the rest is built. Wood is the most common core because it absorbs vibrations. Polyurethane foam instead of wood is sometimes used to make the core. The foam is lighter than wood and is long-lasting. Often a combination of wood, reinforced plastic and foam is used.

Metal, fiberglass or high-tech fibers such as carbon and **Kevlar** are used to cover the core. Carbon fibers make a snowboard strong, while Kevlar reduces the board's weight. Like wood, Kevlar absorbs vibrations and makes for a better, smoother ride.

Building the snowboard

There are three methods of building snowboards:

- cap construction – a one-piece cover is placed over the core to form the top and sidewall
- reaction injection molding (RIM) – a wood core is placed into a mold, and resin is injected into the mold around the core
- laminated construction – multiple layers of one or more materials are glued to a wood or foam core.

Making the signature deck

Many professional snowboarders have their own signature decks. These are decks that have been signed by the snowboarder and are decorated with a graphic design that is unique to them.

Other snowboards come in all the colors of the rainbow. Some are decorated with graphics that have been designed by artists working for the snowboarding companies. There are thousands of different designs.

Bindings and boots

Bindings hold the snowboarder's boots to the snowboard. All bindings are set just past shoulder width and angled gently. They should not be too loose (the board could fly off and cause an accident), or too tight (this would be uncomfortable).

STEP-IN BINDINGS

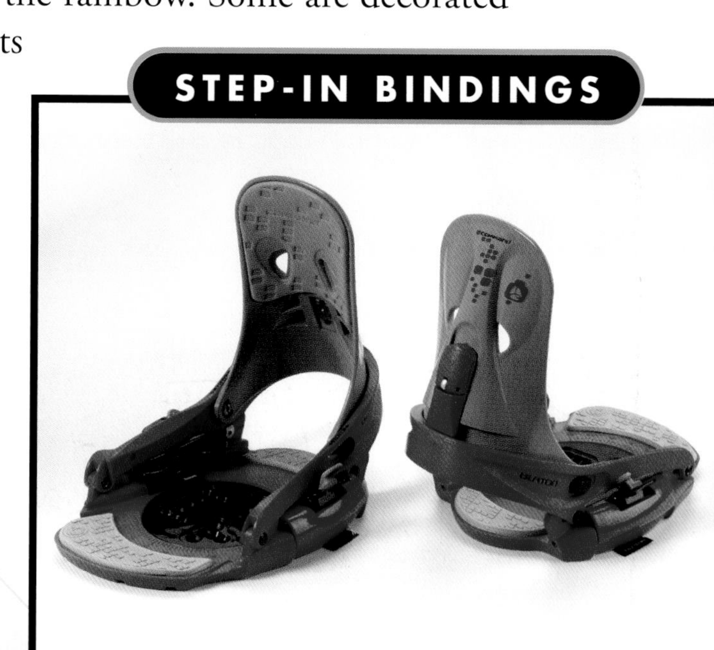

Soft bindings

Soft bindings are used by freestyle and freeriding snowboarders. They are made of strong plastic, metal or carbon fiber. Soft bindings fit over the soft boots with leather uppers and rubber soles that are usually worn by freestyle boarders. The bindings have a calf support at the back and are held in place by buckled straps.

Hard bindings

Racers and snowboarders who want to make high-speed turns use hard bindings. They are made of hard metal or plastic. The bindings fit over the hard ski-type boots that racers wear. They have a metal bail that snaps down on the toe and a heel to fasten the rider to the board.

Step-in bindings

Step-in bindings are quick and easy to use. They are like soft bindings but there is no strap over the boot. These bindings come in several different styles. One way of stepping into the binding is to attach the toe first and then to click down on the heel. Another way is to attach one side of the boot and then the other.

PUTTING ON THE BOARD

The **leash** is attached to the rider's front leg. This stops the board from sliding away and injuring other people. The board is then placed **perpendicular** to the slope. The snowboarder steps into the front binding and fastens the straps. When the front foot is secured, the back foot is placed into the bindings.

SOFT BINDINGS

Other gear

Gloves and wrist guards

To keep their hands warm, snowboarders wear gloves with long cuffs that fit over the sleeves of their jackets. The most common injuries for a snowboarder occur to the thumbs and the wrist.

Gloves worn by freestyle riders are often reinforced with Kevlar. This protects the hands from the sharp, steel edges of the snowboard when performing tricks such as **grabs**. Gloves worn by racers have extra padding across the back and in the wrists. This protects the hands from damage on downhill slalom races through gates. Free riders wear wrist guards or gloves with built-in wrist protection.

Clothes

Clothes are made of material that is hard wearing, lightweight, waterproof and insulated against the cold. Snowboarders usually wear layers of clothes to keep out the cold. The first layer is made of special thermal underwear, usually long johns (underpants with long legs) and a T-shirt.

Special snowboarding pants have built-in padding to protect the knees and the seat. They are long enough to cover the top of the rider's boots and keep out the snow.

The jackets and pants have air vents that can be opened and closed with a zipper. When the snowboarder gets hot, the vents can be opened to let cool air in.

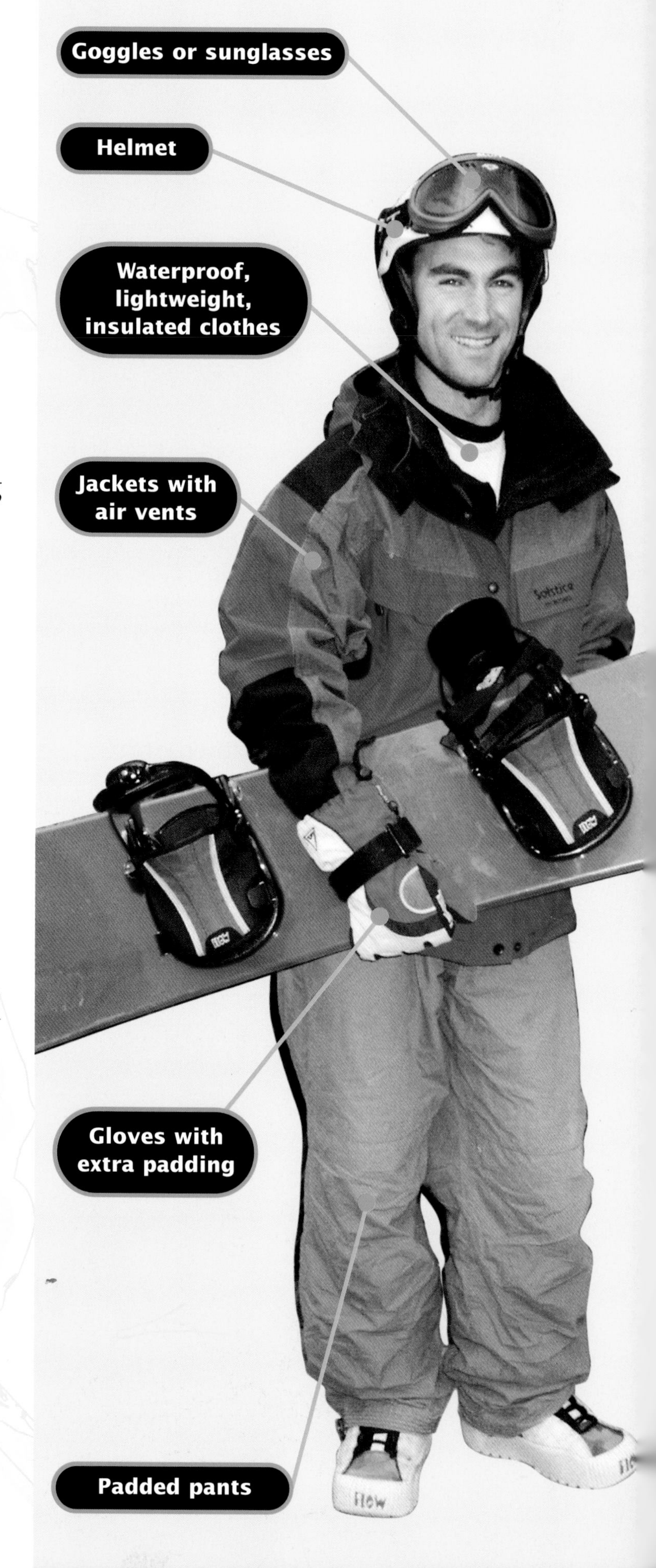

Helmets

Helmets are not usually worn by racers or halfpipe snowboarders, but they are recommended for beginners to protect the head during a fall. Helmets should always be worn by snowboarders tackling obstacle courses and for extreme snowboarding.

Helmets are lightweight and designed to provide protection against the cold snowboarding environment. A snug-fitting helmet will give the best protection. A snowboarder wearing a correctly fitting helmet is safe and comfortable, and can see and hear clearly.

If a rider does not wear a helmet, a wool hat will keep the head warm.

Clothes that are insulated and waterproof keep the wearer warm and comfortable in the snow.

Goggles or sunglasses

Goggles or sunglasses will help a snowboarder see better in the glare of the snow and keep flying snow out of the eyes. They will also protect the rider's eyes from the sun's harmful ultraviolet (UV) rays. Snowboarders prefer plastic lenses because they are lighter and do not break into dangerous splinters like glass lenses.

UV rays are more intense high up a mountain, even on a dull day, so goggles or sunglasses are essential.

SNOWBOARDING SAFELY

Snowboarders should buy a well-made snowboard. A snowboard made of wood and foam will last the longest, and it will be less likely to crack or blow out the steel edges. Bindings are kept in place by bolts. These can pop out of a poorly made board, causing the rider to fall and perhaps be injured.

Obeying the rules

Snowboarding in areas where there are other people nearby is safest.

Snowboarders should follow these basic rules to keep themselves and others safe and injury-free:

- obey rules and signs
- give way to a skier or snowboarder who is farther downhill
- never stop on a slope or below the crest of a hill
- maintain control of the snowboard at all times
- wear a leash to stop the board from sliding away out of control and becoming a free-flying missile
- never ride on slopes that are too difficult for them
- snowboard with a friend or where there are other people
- snowboard within the boundaries of the ski or resort areas
- wear protective clothing and keep warm
- wait their turn in the halfpipe.

Choosing the right trail

Three internationally recognized signs help snowboarders to choose a trail that suits their skill level.

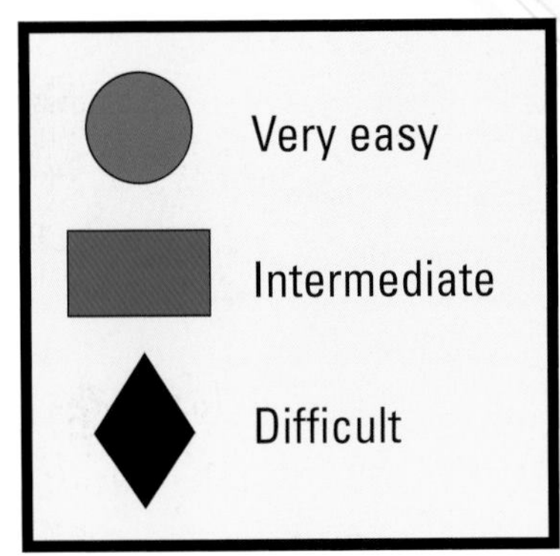

Warming up and keeping fit

Snowboarding is a tough sport and riders need stamina. To build the necessary fitness, many snowboarders run, ride bike or jump rope. Like most sports people, snowboarders warm up before hitting the slopes. They spend a few minutes stretching to warm up the main muscle groups in the legs, back, wrists and shoulders. Walking around or climbing for a few minutes will also warm the snowboarder's muscles. Warm muscles are less likely to cramp in the cold.

ACTION FACT

Hypothermia is an extreme loss of body heat that occurs when a person gets too cold. The person becomes tired, lacks the energy to keep moving, and may collapse.

Wearing the right clothes

Staying warm and dry is essential for successful snowboarding. The wind and wetness in the snow remove body heat faster than the body can produce it. If the body is not kept warm, it will slow down and the snowboarder will lose concentration and energy. Lightweight, waterproof and insulated clothes, along with goggles or sunglasses, should always be worn when snowboarding.

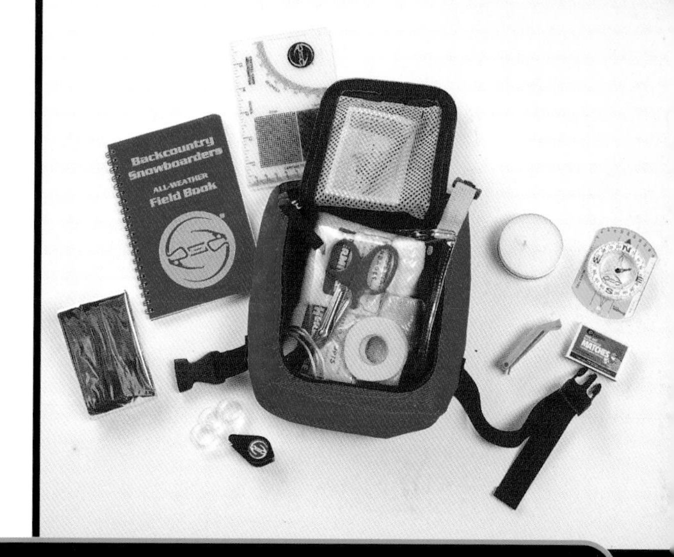

CARRYING EXTRA PROVISIONS

Because they ride in rough country away from the slopes of the resorts, freeriding snowboarders need extra provisions for safety. They need to carry a first-aid kit, food, water, a map and a compass.

Surviving avalanches

Avalanches are huge slabs of snow that fall down a mountain. Snowboarders should carry an avalanche beeper whenever they ride in areas that have steep slopes and are far from regular ski slopes. The beeper will transmit a signal to rescuers if the snowboarder becomes trapped and buried in the snow.

An avalanche can sweep away anything in its path, even cars.

MAINTAINING THE SNOWBOARD

After a day on the snow, the board should be wiped and dried to avoid rusting or warping (bending out of shape). Here are some basic steps that snowboarders should follow to maintain or 'tune' a snowboard for a fast, safe ride.

Filing the edges

Edges grip the snow and help the snowboarder to make turns. If the edges are rounded or burred (rough), they will slip free and make turning difficult. The edges are filed to keep them in good condition.

Preparing the base

The base of the snowboard should be kept as clean and smooth as possible. A cleaning fluid is used to remove dirt from the base. Hot wax is then poured onto the snowboard. When the wax has had a chance to cool a little and be absorbed by the board, the excess is scraped off. Waxing makes the board glide and turn easily across the snow. The wax also seals the board and keeps water out.

Repairing the base

Scratches and gouges in the base slow it down. To keep the snowboard smooth, the base is rubbed with a steel scraper. The scratches are then filled with plastic filler that is dripped into the grooves.

Taking good care of the snowboard ensures that it will perform well in the snow.

Structuring the base

This job is done on a machine in a ski shop. A finely grooved pattern is put into the base of the snowboard to reduce the dragging effect of the snow. The grooves allow air and water to pass under the base without slowing down the snowboard. This procedure is especially important for alpine racers and slalom riders, who want a high-speed board.

The snowboarder's repair kit

Snowboarders often carry tools with them to perform minor repairs. Some basic tools and materials needed to tune the board are:

- base cleaner and a cloth
- brass and nylon brushes to clean out gouges
- edge file
- plastic scraper to remove excess wax
- polishing stones used after filing the edges
- bullet tool
- P-Tex (a plastic filler).

The bullet tool is used to help tighten or loosen screws and bolts.

SKILLS, TRICKS AND TECHNIQUES

The basics

Beginner snowboarders should start out on a gentle hill rather than a mountain.

Standing on the board

The first thing a snowboarder learns is how to stand on the board. There are two positions:

- regular foot is when the left foot is forward and pointed toward the front of the board, with the right foot behind
- goofy foot is when the right foot is forward and the left foot behind.

The correct position is the one that feels most comfortable.

The snowboarder must also learn how to slide on the board using the edges to catch or slice through the snow. Staying balanced while crouching down and standing up on the board must be learned as well.

FRONTSIDE TURN

The snowboarder looks in the direction of the turn and puts weight onto the toe edge. The board starts to turn. The rider bends the knees and steers the board by turning the hips, shoulders and arms while pushing down gently on the back leg. To stop a turn, the snowboarder straightens up and shifts weight from the toe edge to the center of the board.

Turning (carving)

Turning controls the speed of the snowboard. Turns are made by putting pressure on either the **toe edge** or **heel edge** of the board. There are two basic turns:

- frontside turn – where the rider turns on the toe edge, facing the turn
- heelside turn – where the rider turns on the heel edge, with their back to the turn.

HEELSIDE TURN

The snowboarder looks over the front shoulder in the direction of the turn and puts weight onto the heel edge. The board starts to turn. The rider then bends the knees and steers the board by pushing down gently on the back leg.

Stopping

A snowboarder stops by turning sharply to either the left or right, bringing both feet perpendicular to the slope and scraping to a stop. As the turn is made, the rider puts pressure on either the toe edge or heel edge, depending on the direction of the turn. This makes the edge dig deeper into the snow.

The easiest way for a beginner to stop is to sit down and slide a little.

STOPPING

Learning to fall

All snowboarders fall over at some time. Knowing how to fall helps a snowboarder avoid injuries.

If falling forwards, snowboarders should clench their fists and put their arms out in front to land on the forearms. This avoids a broken or sprained wrist. These are the most common injuries for snowboarders, especially those who are learning.

If falling backwards, snowboarders should let their seat hit the snow first, and then slide to a stop. Their arms and hands should be stretched out in front of their bodies to avoid injury.

FALLING

Beyond the basics

Sideslipping

There are two types of sideslips:

- on the toe edge, when the rider balances on the balls of both feet while keeping the knees bent
- on the heel edge, when the rider balances on the heels.

Traversing

Traversing is riding across the **fall line** from one side to the other, zigzagging gently down a hill. To traverse, the snowboarder begins a toe edge sideslip, then turns to face the direction they want to move in. The weight is shifted to the front foot, and the back foot steers the board as it moves across the slope of the hill. Traversing can be done **fakie**, when the rider leads with the back foot by putting weight on it.

Sideslipping occurs when the snowboarder skids straight downhill by the fall line.

Fall line

Traversing

TRAVERSING

The ollie

The ollie is a basic snowboarding jump. It is named after the famous skateboarder, Alan 'Ollie' Gelfand, who invented it in the mid-1970s. To perform an ollie, the snowboarder moves in a straight line, then rocks back on the snowboard so that all the weight is on the back foot. Then the snowboarder jumps forward, from the tail of the board. The snowboarder tries to land the board flat, so that as much of the board hits the snow or surface as possible. The knees are bent and arms stretched out for balance. After landing the board, the snowboarder rides off.

Grabs

Grabs can be added to the ollie. While in the air, the rider bends the knees and reaches down to grab the board. The trick has different names, depending on which hand is used and which edge is grabbed. For example, an indie is when the back hand is used to grab the toe edge, between the rider's legs. If the heel edge is grabbed, with the front hand between the rider's legs, it is called a chicken salad.

Rail grinding

Rail grinding is when a snowboarder jumps onto a railing, the edge of a table or a bench, and rides along it. The trick is named according to which part of the snowboard is touching the railing. For example, a 50-50 has the snowboard **parallel** to the railing. A board slide has the snowboard across the rail.

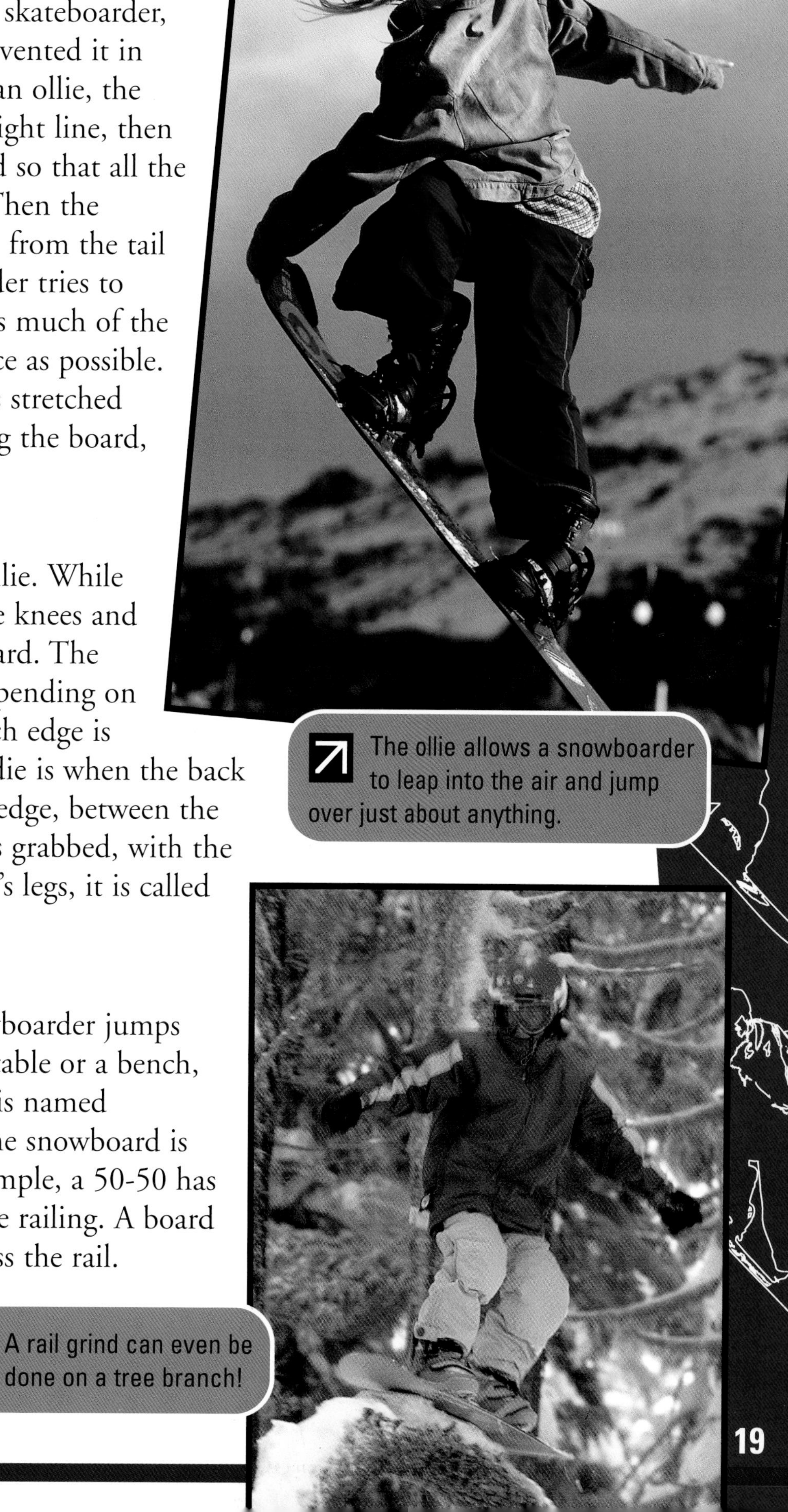

The ollie allows a snowboarder to leap into the air and jump over just about anything.

A rail grind can even be done on a tree branch!

Getting started in the halfpipe

The halfpipe is a U-shaped trench in the snow. A halfpipe can be between 50 and 100 meters long, and 10 and 18 meters wide. The walls can be between 1.5 meters and 3 meters high, with a platform or deck at least 1 meter wide. The curved section between the flat at the bottom of the halfpipe and the flat part of the wall is called the transition.

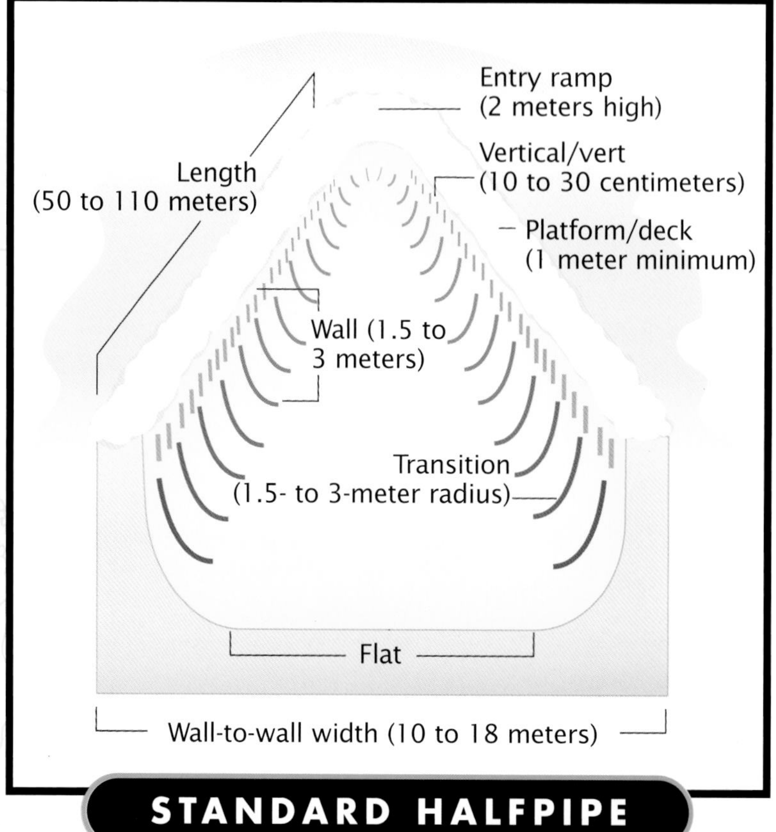

STANDARD HALFPIPE

Basic moves in the halfpipe

The first thing a rider learns in the halfpipe is traversing. This is riding across the pipe from side to side, forwards and backwards.

Next come side turns. Here the snowboarder rides up to the top of the wall, turns and rides down the wall.

The first **air** in the halfpipe is the bunny-hop. The rider gets to the top of the halfpipe wall, and hops a little to become airborne as the turn is made.

ALLEY OOP

This is a spin trick. The snowboarder here is building up enough speed to make it up the wall. At the top, the rider will jump into the air, spinning 180 degrees. When the turn is completed, the rider will land and ride away.

FRONTSIDE OR TOESIDE GRAB

This is an air with grab trick. While in the air, the rider grabs the toe edge with the back hand.

LAYBACK AIR

This is a handplant trick. The snowboarder rides up the wall. As their front foot passes the **lip**, the snowboarder reaches back and plants a hand on the lip. The board then shoots over the rider's head.

Freeriding

Freeriding is done away from the groomed slopes and ski slopes of a resort. The freeriding snowboarder travels over rough country, through treed areas and in deep **powder snow**. On their way down a mountain, freeriding snowboarders jump and turn, drop off cliffs, and ride down the steep slopes of mountain gullies and other narrow passages, known as chutes.

A SNOWBOARDING INTERVIEW

Marcus Zeuschner is a snowboarder who has ridden in Australia, Austria, Switzerland and Canada.

How long have you been a snowboarder?

I first tried snowboarding 11 years ago but didn't take to it seriously until three years ago. I switched from skiing then.

MARCUS ZEUSCHNER

Why did you take it up as a sport?

I went to live in Austria and I saw the possibilities for freeriding there and in other parts of Europe. Within a week I had experienced waist-deep powder snow and although I was still falling over fairly regularly, I was hooked.

Why do you like the freeriding style?

I enjoy the freedom and the adventure of riding **off-piste**. It's because the sport combines the challenges of mountaineering with the rush of dropping steep chutes, cliff drops and open terrain. It's also away from the lines and crowds of the ski resorts.

What sort of people snowboard?

I've seen people of all different ages snowboarding although most of them are younger than 50. Once, in Switzerland, I saw a 4-year-old who was getting half a meter (a foot and a half) of air outside the pipe. The sport is really growing but there are usually more males than females.

What's the atmosphere like on the slopes?

Ten years ago, snowboarders weren't treated well at the resorts but the attitudes to us have slowly changed. There's a friendly rivalry now between skiers and snowboarders and this is good because it's leading to new developments in the sport, for example bigger jumps and harder tricks.

Marcus Zeuschner in action.

How safe is snowboarding?

Snowboarding is a safe sport as long as you follow the rules for keeping safe. Having the right gear and behaving sensibly on the snow will make sure you have an exciting, adventurous and safe time. My rule is 'respect the mountain and it will respect you'.

What about avalanches?

Avalanches are a serious hazard for snowboarders like myself who go freeriding. However, I always carry an avalanche 'bleeps device' and never ride alone. With proper training and common sense, you learn to minimize the risks.

Have you ever experienced an avalanche?

Yes. I've been in two. Despite all your efforts, sometimes things go wrong. My experience of avalanches was that they are similar to being dumped by a large wave in the surf. There are many ideas about what you should do if caught, but all I can say is I fought like mad to stay on top.

How can people find out about the snowboarding scene?

Well, there are books like this one written about snowboarding and there are others which tell how to do it. I also read magazines about the sport and the internet has quite a few sites about snowboarding. There are videos too, showing top riders in action.

IN COMPETITION

Snowboarding competitions are friendly contests where people show off their new tricks. Professional snowboarders travel to various parts of the world to compete for prize money in snowboarding competitions. Judging is done according to the rules of the International Snowboard Federation (ISF) or the United States Snowboarding Association (USSA).

Halfpipe competitions

Competitors drop-in to the halfpipe and then perform tricks off the walls of the pipe. Loud music and high spirits accompany the events.

A halfpipe competitor at the Winter Olympics.

ISF rules

Judges award points in three areas:

- amplitude – the height above the platform that is reached by the rider
- execution – the style of the rider. The judges look for a free-flowing series of tricks
- variety – the number of tricks, frontside and backside, that the rider performs during the routine.

USSA rules

Judges award points in five areas:

- amplitude • difficulty • landings • style • variety.

Alpine racing competitions

Alpine racing includes slalom, giant slalom and super G. These events differ in the slope of the course, the number of gates, and the distance the gates are set apart. Competitors race down a slope, weaving in and out of the poles, called gates. The fastest rider is the winner.

Dual slalom competitors race each other in pairs.

SNOWBOARDING CHAMPIONS

Snowboarding competitions began in the 1980s. At first, snowboarders had to compete with skiers for space on the mountains and for sponsors. Snowboarding was not considered a serious competitive sport. By behaving responsibly, respecting the environment, abiding by the rules and the judges' decisions, competitive snowboarders soon gained the respect and admiration of spectators and promoters of competitions. International snowboarding events in Japan, Europe and the United States draw huge crowds. Champions of the sport are now able to compete at the Winter Olympics.

↗ Terje Haakonsen

- Halfpipe snowboarder
- Born October 11, 1974
- Lives in Norway
- Began snowboarding in 1990

Career highlights

- Invented a trick called the Haakon flip
- European Halfpipe Champion 1991–1994, 1997
- World Cup Halfpipe Champion 1992, 1994
- World Halfpipe Champion 1993, 1995, 1997
- United States Open Halfpipe Champion 1992, 1993, 1995
- Mt. Baker Banked Slalom Champion 1995, 1996, 1998
- Nippon Open Champion 1999

↗ Shaun Palmer

- Snowboards in many styles including boardercross, halfpipe, downhill slalom and freestyle
- Born November 14, 1968
- Lives in South Lake Tahoe, California
- Began snowboarding in 1982
- Began competing in 1985

Career highlights

- Invented a trick called the Palm air
- Has been a world champion snowboarder five times
- First overall winner in the Swatch World Tour, 1996 and 1997
- First in the boardercross at the ESPN X Games, 1998

↗ Ross Rebagliati

- Alpine snowboarder
- Born July 14, 1971
- Lives in British Columbia, Canada

Career highlights

- Became the only non-European to win the European Championships, in 1994
- Gold medal Nagano Olympic Games, 1998

↗ Shannon Dunn

- Freestyle snowboarder
- Born November 26, 1972
- Lives in California
- Began snowboarding at 15 (skied from the age of three)

Career highlights

- U.S. Open Halfpipe Champion, 1993 and 1994
- Winter Olympic bronze medallist in the halfpipe, 1998
- Three Grand Prix halfpipe wins in competitions in the United States, 2000
- Second at U.S. Open Championships, 2000
- Second at Nippon Open Championships, 2000
- First place women's superpipe competition at the Winter X Games, 2001
- Fifth place women's superpipe competition at the Winter X Games, 2002

↗ Ross Powers

- Halfpipe snowboarder
- Born February 10, 1979
- Lives in Vermont
- Began competing in 1996

Career highlights

- First FIS World Halfpipe Champion, 1997
- Won the bronze medal at the Nagano Olympic Games in halfpipe, 1998
- FIS World Cup Overall Halfpipe Champion, 1999
- Third place USSA Grand Prix Halfpipe, 1999
- U.S. Open Halfpipe Champion, 1999
- Firsts in the Gravity Games and the Goodwill Games, 2000
- Second place in the U.S. Open, the X Games and the Tahoe Grand Prix in 2000
- Overall ISF World Halfpipe Champion, 2000
- Third place Men's Snowboard Super-Pipe at the Winter X Games, 2001
- Gold medal at the Salt Lake City Olympic Games in halfpipe, 2002
- Won the halfpipe competition at the U.S. Open Snowboarding Championship, 2003

↗ Karine Ruby

- Giant slalom snowboarder
- Born January 4, 1978
- Lives in Chamonix, France
- Began competing in 1994

Career highlights

- Won the giant slalom at the World Championships, 1996
- Boardercross World Champion, 1997
- Second in the giant slalom at the World Championships, 1997
- Won the gold medal in the giant slalom at the Nagano Olympic Games, 1998
- Second in overall rankings of the World Cup, 1999
- Second place in the World Cup Parallel Giant Slalom, 2001

1929–1998 THEN AND NOW

1929	1963	1965	Late 1960s	1970
M.J. 'Jack' Burchett makes one of the first skis by cutting out a plank of plywood and securing his feet to it with some rope and horse reins.	American teenager Tom Sims constructed a ski board for his class project by changing his skateboard so it could be used on snow. Tom later became a top snowboarder and skateboarder.	Sherman Poppen from Michigan invented the Snurfer as a toy for his children.	Snurfers were banned from ski areas because they were uncontrollable. Snowboarders were forced to use slopes and trails away from the main ski slopes.	Dimitrije Milovich, an American surfer, decided it would be fun to slide down mountain slopes on cafeteria trays. He did so and then went on to develop his own snowboard.

Late 1960s

1975

The March edition of *Newsweek* magazine contained an article about Milovich and his snowboard, which he called a Winterstick.

1978

Jake Burton Carpenter, a famous snowboarder, opened the first snowboard factory. Jake also convinced some ski resorts to allow snowboards onto the slopes. Burton boards are now one of the most famous snowboard brands.

1982

The first international snowboard race was held at Suicide Six, just outside Woodstock, New York.

1985

Absolute Radical, the first magazine about snowboarding, began publishing.

1989

Professional snowboarders competed for prize money and the sport was shown on television.

An International Snowboarding Federation was established. Competitions were held in Japan, Europe and the United States.

1998

Snowboarding became a sport at the Winter Olympics in Nagano, Japan. Two events were included: the downhill slalom and the halfpipe competition.

1978

RELATED ACTION SPORTS

World Extreme Championships

This event is held each year in Alaska. Competitors are dropped off on top of a mountain and then find their way down, one at a time. The judges award points in six areas:

- aggressiveness or attack – how energetically the contestant rides
- form – the rider's style
- fluidity – the pace and smoothness of the rider's movements
- air – how well the rider jumps and performs the take-offs and landings
- difficulty of the moves
- control – keeping in touch with the board and not falling or, if falling, how well the rider recovers.

BOARDERCROSS

Boardercross

This sport combines freestyle snowboarding, racing and jumping. Six riders race along a course with jumps, **banked turns** and slalom gates. Riders may jostle each other for front position, but a rider can be disqualified if the jostling turns into bumping.

GLOSSARY

airs tricks performed while the snowboarder is airborne

amateur an athlete who has never competed for money

banked turns long piles of snow which snowboarders turn along

fakie riding backwards

fall line the direct route straight down a mountain

grabs tricks in which the rider grabs either edge of the snowboard with one or both hands while airborne

halfpipe a U-shaped snow structure built for freestyle snowboarding

heel edge the edge of the snowboard at which the rider's heels rest

Kevlar an artificial material that is extremely strong and heat-resistant

leash a device used to attach the snowboard to the front foot so that it does not get away from the rider

lip the top of the wall of the halfpipe

nose the front tip of the snowboard

off-piste places that are not marked as resort trails or slopes; a place for freeriding

parallel running in the same direction while staying a fixed distance from something, such as a railing

perpendicular at right angles

powder snow soft, deep, ungroomed snow

slalom a downhill race in which the racers zigzag in and around obstacles

toe edge the edge of the snowboard closest to the rider's toes

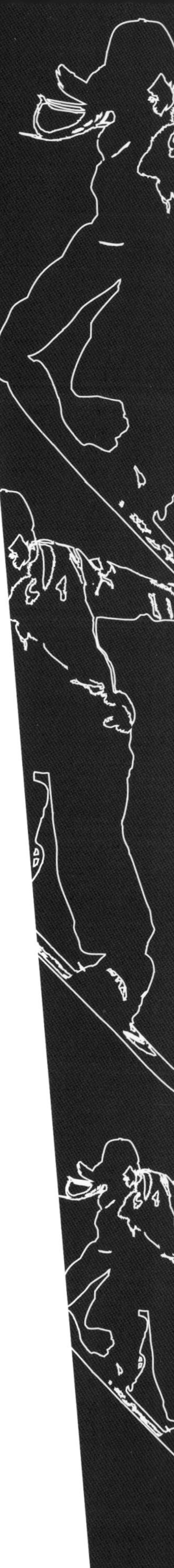

INDEX